Shaping Materials

SQUASH IT!

by Tammy Enz

capstone

© 2018 Heinemann Raintree
an imprint of Capstone Global Library, LLC
Chicago, Illinois

To contact Capstone Global Library, please call 800-747-4992,
or visit our web site www.capstonepub.com

Edited by Linda Staniford
Designed by Kayla Rossow
Original illustrations © Capstone Global Library Limited 2018
Picture research by Kelli Lageson
Production by Victoria Fitzgerald
Originated by Capstone Global Library Ltd

21 20 19 18 17
10 9 8 7 6 5 4 3 2 1

Library of Congress Cataloging-in-Publication Data
Library of Congress Cataloging-in-Publication Data is available on the Library of Congress website.
ISBN: 978-1-4846-4095-1 (library hardcover)
ISBN: 978-1-4846-4099-9 (paperback)
ISBN: 978-1-4846-4104-0 (eBook PDF)

This book has been officially leveled using the F&P Text Level Gradient™ Leveling System.

Acknowledgments
We would like to thank the following for permission to reproduce photographs: Capstone Studio: Karon Dubke, cover, 1, 8, 9, 12, 13, 16, 17, 18, 18, 19, 22, (bottom left and middle left); iStockphoto: ChiccoDodiFC, 5, Niran_pr, 14, 22, (bottom left); Shutterstock: Africa Studio, 21, Alim Yakubov, 10, 22, (top left) Artem Shadrin, back cover, 11, aza_za, 6, 22, (top right), ber1a, throughout (background), David Papazian, 21, itakdalee, 15, Natasha R. Graham, cover (background), SUWIT NGAOKAEW, back cover, 7, Verkhovynets Taras, 4, 22, (top right), Werayuth Tes, 20

Every effort has been made to contact copyright holders of material reproduced in this book. Any omissions will be rectified in subsequent printings if notice is given to the publisher.

Printed and bound in China
PO010438F17

Table of Contents

Some words are shown in bold, **like this**.
You can find out what they mean by looking
in the glossary.

What Is Squashable?

Squash! Squish! Crush! Mash!
Many things can be squashed.
When you squash an object,
you change its shape or **form**.

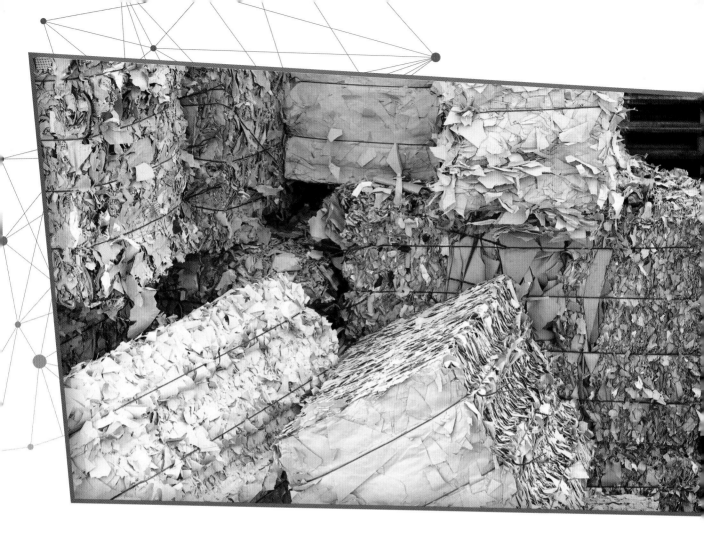

Soft materials squash easily.
It's harder to squash things like
wood or concrete. Some materials
stay squashed. Some spring back.
Others break apart.

Materials That Spring Back

Some things squash easily. They are called **elastic**. But they don't stay that way. They spring back to their original shape.

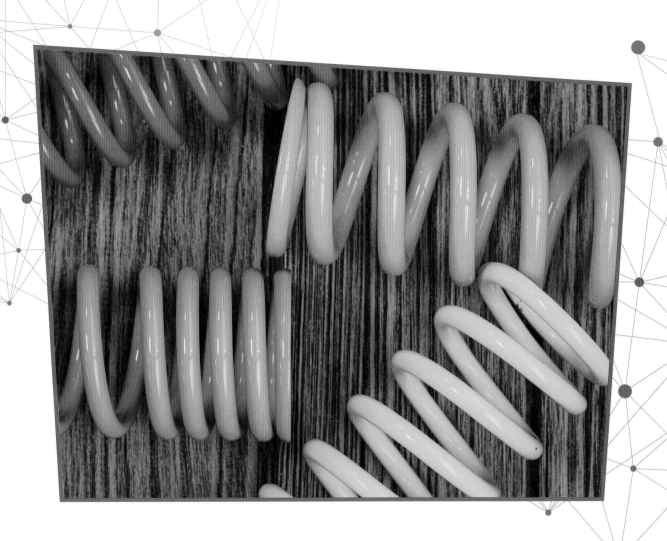

Things like pillows, carpet,
and foam spring back.
Marshmallows spring back
when squashed.
Coils and springs are elastic too.

Project:
Squish-Squash Game

Squash foam and see it spring back to its original shape.

You Will Need:

- Piece of paper
- Marker
- 10 foam earplugs (5 of each color)
- 2 players

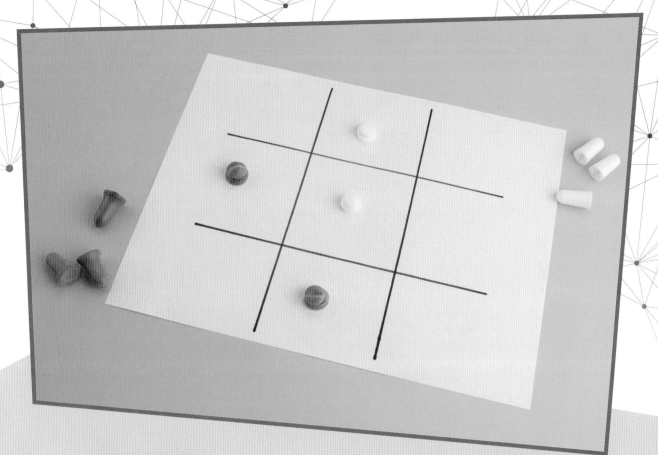

What To Do:

1. Draw a tic-tac-toe grid on the paper.
2. Each player chooses a color.
3. Take turns pressing an earplug into a square.
4. The first to place three in a row of one color wins. (They can be up, down, or diagonal too.)
5. Play quickly. If all your plugs pop up, you lose!
6. See how the earplugs pop back to their original shape.

Materials That Squash and Stay

Not all squashed materials go back to their original shape. Some objects keep the squashed shape.

These materials change their shape or form when squashed. Squash some dough. Squish your mashed potatoes. These things get shorter when squashed. They also get wider. Their form changes.

Project:
Squash Monster

See how clay changes its form.

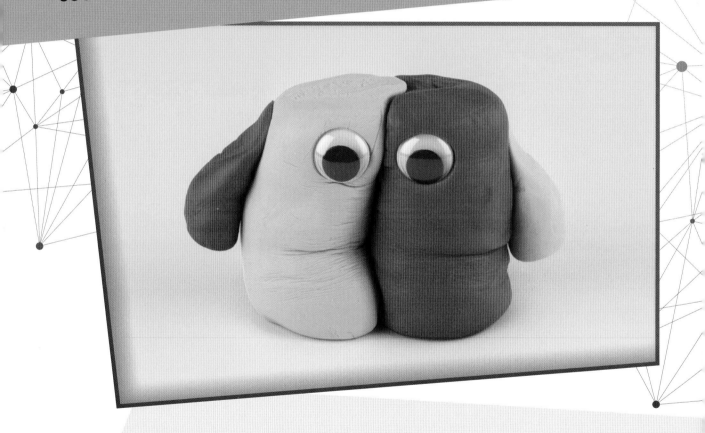

You Will Need:

- 2 different colors of playdough or clay
- 2 googly eyes

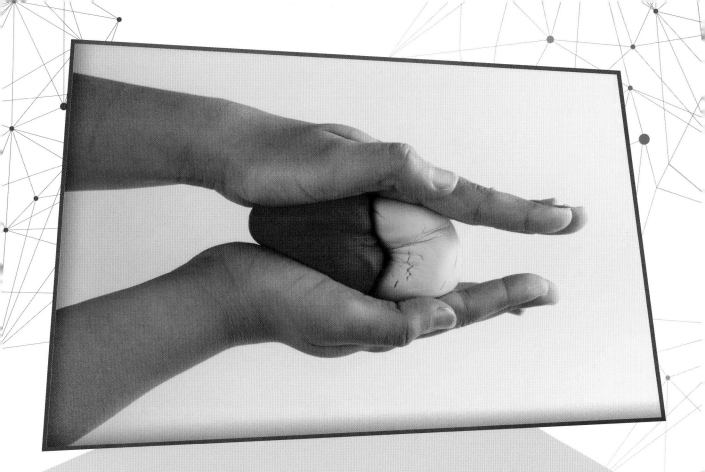

What To Do:

1. Roll each piece of dough into a log. Save a small piece of each color to make the arms (step 4).
2. Place the logs next to each other and stand them on one end.
3. Squash both logs, but not completely flat.
4. Add arms and eyes. Allow to dry.
5. See how the clay holds its new shape.

Materials That Squash and Shatter

The size of some materials changes when squashed or broken. These things have pockets of air or water inside. The water or air leaks out when these things are squashed.

A piece of cake is filled with tiny air bubbles. It gets smaller when you squash it.

Project: Cereal Crush

Cereal is full of air pockets called **voids**. When you squash cereal, the air pockets disappear. Now the cereal takes up less space.

You Will Need:

- 2 cups of dry flaked or puffed grain cereal
- 1 large self-sealing plastic bag

What To Do:

1. Place the cereal from one cup in the bag. Seal.
2. Crush and pound the cereal until it becomes powdery.
3. Pour back into the cup.
4. Compare the two cups. What happened?

Project: Squash Art

Squashing berries releases the liquid inside. This liquid can **stain** paper. Fruits and berries are often used to make dye for coloring cloth. Try this project to see what happens when berries are squashed.

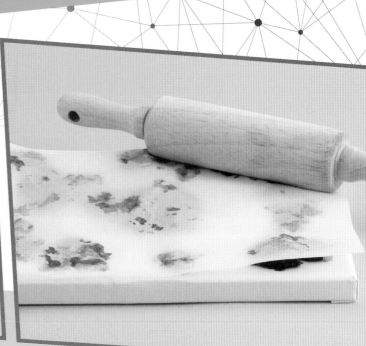

You Will Need:

- Thick art paper or a paint canvas
- 2 different kinds of canned or fresh berries (blueberries, blackberries or raspberries)
- Waxed paper
- Rolling pin

What To Do:

1. Use a handful of each type of berries. Make a design on the paper.
2. Cover it with a sheet of waxed paper.
3. Crush the berries with the rolling pin.
4. Remove the waxed paper.
5. Wait one hour. Scrape away the berry pieces to see your art.
6. See how the juice inside the berries has leaked out. What has happened to the berries?

You Squash It!

Some things squash. Some don't.
Try squashing and squishing
materials around you.

Find things that spring back. Find things that don't. What kinds of materials squash and shatter?

Picture Glossary

form   shape

elastic   able to stretch out and return to its original size and shape

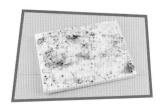

stain   to mark or discolor something

void   an empty space

Find Out More

Jenner, Caryn. *Materials.* Play and Discover.
London, U.K.: Franklin Watts, 2014.

Jiang, Helga. *Clay Charm Magic!*
New York, N.Y.: Sky Pony Press, 2014.

Peppas, Lynn. *How Do We Measure Matter?*
Matter Close-Up. New York, N.Y.: Crabtree, 2012.

Rompella, Natalie. *Experiments in Material
and Matter with Toys and Everyday Stuff.*
Fun Science. Mankato, Minn.: Capstone, 2015.

Use FactHound to find Internet sites
related to this book.

Visit *www.facthound.com*

Just type in 9781484640951 and go!

Check out projects, games and lots more at
www.capstonekids.com

Index

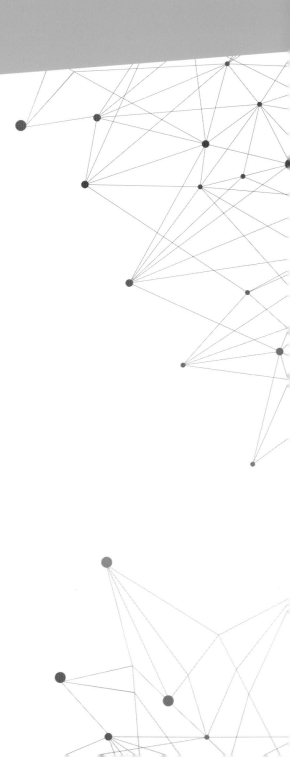